Reckoning

Reckoning

An ARTICLE 11 work by

Tara Beagan and Andy Moro

Reckoning
first published 2016 by
Scirocco Drama
An imprint of J. Gordon Shillingford Publishing Inc.

Scirocco Drama Editor: Glenda MacFarlane
Cover design by Doowah Design Inc. and Andy Moro
Front cover photo of John Ng
Back cover photo of Jonathan Fisher
Cover photo and interior production photos by Luca Caruso-Moro
Author photos by Andy Moro

Printed and bound in Canada on 100% post-consumer recycled paper.

We acknowledge the financial support of the Manitoba Arts Council
and The Canada Council for the Arts for our publishing program.

Production inquiries,
please contact the playwrights at
tb@article11.ca or am@article11.ca

Library and Archives Canada Cataloguing in Publication

Beagan, Tara, author
Reckoning / Tara Beagan and Andy Moro.

Plays.
Contents: Witness -- Daughter -- Survivor.
ISBN 978-1-927922-26-2 (paperback)

I. Moro, Andy, author II. Title.

PS8603.E34R43 2016 C812'.6 C2016-906478-6

J. Gordon Shillingford Publishing
P.O. Box 86, RPO Corydon Avenue, Winnipeg, MB Canada R3M 3S3

This work is dedicated to all survivors
of attempted genocide who have somehow
kept the courage to love.

This is dedicated to all those we lost to
the Residential Schools and to the
Truth and Reconciliation process,
and whose reconciliation will never come.

We work to offer our healing to you.

Tara Beagan

Tara writes, directs, produces and acts in theatre. She grew up in a story-loving home. Her Ntlaka'pamux mom has always been an avid reader, and her Irish-Canadian dad took her to the library weekly. Her older sister Rebecca (now a teacher) taught her the alphabet after learning it in kindergarten, and her younger brother Patrick (lighting designer / theatre administrator) created worlds and characters with her, sharing an interest in enacting stories. She is a proud auntie to Diana and Owen. Tara is now happy in work with her love, Andy Moro, co-helming Indigenous Arts Activist Company ARTICLE 11. More work credits can be found at tarabeagan.com

Andy Moro

Andy is a multi-award winning Euro/Omushkego Cree designer based in Toronto. Andy co-creates and "designaturges" with companies across Turtle Island, including works in progress with Kaha:wi Dance Theatre in Toronto, Red Sky Performance at the Banff Centre, and the Gitxsan Dancers of Damelahamid in Vancouver. Moro has also been core creative faculty for the Indigenous Dance Residency at Banff since 2012, where he has co-created with Taane Mete, Neil Iremia, Jock Soto, Lina Cruz and more. Andy has twice been named among the Top Ten Theatre Artists in Toronto's *NOW* magazine.

ARTICLE 11

ARTICLE 11 is helmed by Andy Moro and Tara Beagan. Founded in 2013, ARTICLE 11 channels Moro and Beagan's mutual desire to pursue the creation of live performance works with a holistic approach and a rigorous attack. The company is named for the 11th Article of the United Nations Declaration on the Rights of Indigenous Peoples.

"Indigenous peoples have the right to practise and revitalize their cultural traditions and customs. This includes the right to maintain, protect and develop the past, present and future manifestations of their cultures, such as archaeological and historical sites, artifacts, designs, ceremonies, technologies and visual and performing arts and literature."

ARTICLE 11's performative installation *DECLARATION* has been featured at the National Arts Centre and the Royal Ontario Museum and will be presented in Calgary at One Yellow Rabbit's High Performance Rodeo and MT Space's IMPACT in 2017. *In Spirit*, a theatrical work told from the perspective of a missing girl, has partnered with the University of Regina, GTNT, Ryerson University, Queen's University, and will partner with Urban Indigenous Theatre in Winnipeg in 2017. Video Installation project *RUN* was part of The Mush Hole Project at one of this country's oldest Residential Schools, in September 2016.

In April 2016, ARTICLE 11 premiered *Reckoning*—an interdisciplinary triptych tackling layers of fallout from the Truth and Reconciliation Commission. Karen Fricker wrote: "Its excellence sets the bar high… *Reckoning* demonstrates the unique work that live performance can do in bringing people together to share experience, raise awareness, and consider where each of us stands in the still-unfolding story of Canada's relationship to First Peoples." *Toronto Star*, April 17, 2016. *Reckoning*'s Western Canada debut was presented in Edmonton at Fringe Theatre Adventures as part of their 2017/18 season.

Production History

ARTICLE 11 produced the world premiere of *Reckoning* in April of 2016 at the Theatre Centre in Toronto, Ontario, Canada. Toronto is on the traditional territory of the Anishnaabe, Haudenosaunee, and the Huron / Wendat.

Director of performance .... Tara Beagan
Director of design .... Andy Moro

Section 1: Witness

Witness .... John Ng

Section 2: Daughter

Shannon .... PJ Prudat
Emmett .... Glen Gould
Recorded voice of Neighbour .... Andy Moro

Section 3: Survivor

Survivor .... Jonathan Fisher
Recorded voice of Chuck .... Jesse Wabegijig
Recorded voice of Trina .... Lena Recollet

Music composition .... Melody McKiver
Elder research collaborator .... Paul Chaput
Fight choreographer .... Casey Hudecki

Administrating producer ... Leslie Kachena McCue
Production stage manager .... Brittany Ryan

The work addresses graphically violent historical and sexual content. The creators believe support workers and traditional medicines must be on hand for those survivors who may be triggered by the content. For the premiere, support was generously coordinated by Jeff D'Hondt.

Acknowledgements

Special thanks to Brandon Oakes, whose beautiful energy within the role of "Emmett" launched the rehearsal process, and who gave his blessing to have Glen Gould proceed when he could not. Our prayers and love are with you and Anagonse Teiotsirathe, always.

Thanks also to workshop actors Michael Greyeyes and Jonathan Fisher who helped shape "Emmett" immeasurably. Lina Cruz collaborated on initial explorations of *Witness*, and some of the work created with her remained in the final production.

Initial writing of this work was prompted by an invitation extended to Beagan to participate in Wrecking Ball, 2008. The first draft of *Daughter* was written. The work was set aside on sound advice from director Weyni Mengesha, who recognized that the content was too fraught to be shaped as art at that time. Several years later, Beagan was granted support through the OAC's TCR program, thanks to support by fu-GEN and Great Canadian Theatre Company. Beagan and Moro founded ARTICLE 11 in 2013 and Moro was taken by the short script. Through conversations, ARTICLE 11 outlined the remaining two sections of the triptych. Casting and collaboration in studio in 2015 brought the full piece to fruition, with support from the OAC's Aboriginal Arts Program.

Support for production came through the TAC's Indigenous Arts Project and the Canada Council's Theatre Projects programs. We are grateful to the artists who served on these juries and to the officers at these organizations for their work. Leslie Kachena McCue's presence was made possible through the Canada Council's Developmental Support to Aboriginal Theatre Organizations program, which has since been discontinued.

The text heard in the sound score for *Witness* is exact wording that appears in two sources: an official document titled Schedule "D" (draft of 2006), provided to Adjudicators of the IAP, and the Application for the IAP (draft of April 2013) intended for survivors.

Cast

Section 1: Witness

An Independent Assessment Hearings Officer; older than forty, younger than sixty. This man emigrated to Canada at a young age, and is not white.

Section 2: Daughter

Shannon: A mixed blood woman who identifies strongly as Indigenous. She is in her mid-to-late thirties, affluent, and well educated.

Emmett: An Indigenous man who survived several years at Residential School. A lawyer and community advocate.

Section 3: Survivor

An Indigenous man in his fifties who survived all of his school years at Residential School. Adept with technology, he furthered his education and conquered alcoholism while incarcerated.

Setting and Time

Section 1: Witness is in a sparse office in 2010*

Section 2: Daughter is in a condominium downtown in a Canadian city, in 2008*

Section 3: Survivor is in a home on reserve in 2015

*These times can flex earlier or later by a year and maintain accuracy.

The reference to a major park (in the premiere Toronto's "High Park") should be altered to be in the nearest major city where the show is playing.

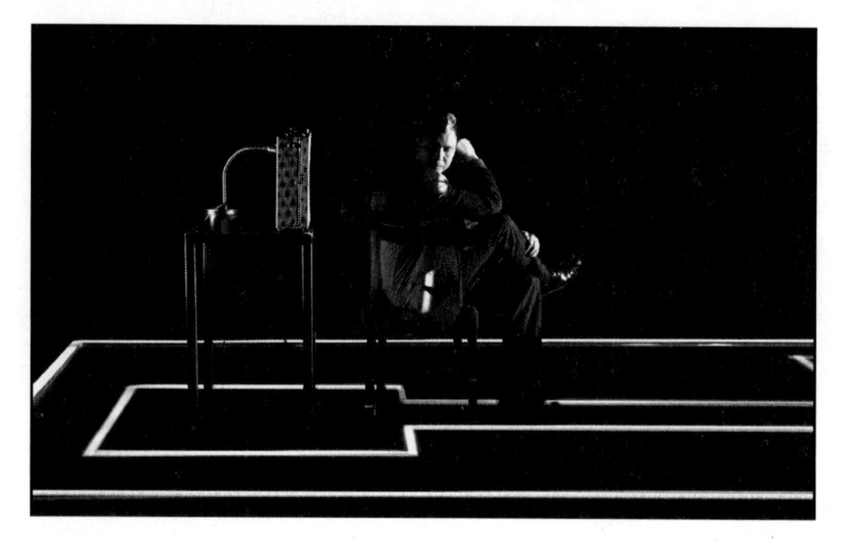

John Ng in *Witness*.

The stage is a space unto its own—a pristine platform. It seems completely separate from the venue itself. Its surface is a simple, flawless grey. Lit from below during pre-show and in transitions, it seems it does not touch venue walls or venue floors. It floats, groundless and apart.

Section 1: Witness

NOTE: All recorded voiceover is in the voice of the performer. Often, there is movement during V/O. When stillness is crucial, it is noted.

Lights bright in the house, pre-show music still playing as the performer emerges, not in character.

A projected title appears above him: "Witness."

As he lands just upstage of the playing platform, the pre-show music fades very quickly.

The performer beholds the audience.

He adjusts his tie.

Quick blackout.

He crosses to the stage, sounds of shoes clacking on hard floor. We hear him pick up a briefcase and arrive at stillness.

V/O: *(in darkness)* "INDEPENDENT ASSESSMENT PROCESS (IAP) FOR CONTINUING INDIAN RESIDENTIAL SCHOOL ABUSE CLAIMS"

Lights and music up, actor is now in character.

V/O: "CRITERIA FOR THE SELECTION OF ADJUDICATORS

—Law degree from a recognized university. Consideration will also be given to candidates with a combination of related training and/or significant experience.

—Knowledge of and sensitivity to Aboriginal culture and history.

—Knowledge of and sensitivity to sexual and physical abuse issues."

He looks to the mirror opposite the doorway—it is the fourth wall.

He looks to chair at the desk and then down to the briefcase in his hands.

He looks back to the mirror.

He takes two steps into the room and turns his body towards the chair/desk.

He reaches with his far arm toward the chair/desk, trying to will himself to get down to work.

He stops reaching and lands his feet side by side, shifting the plane of his body to face the chair/desk fully.

He breathes deep, lifting his head to the sky. In this he makes a decision.

He takes three measured steps toward the chair/desk and swings his briefcase onto the seat of the chair.

He nudges the chair closer to the desk.

He crouches slowly to lift the case as though it is loaded with explosives, setting it carefully on the desk, upright.

The presence of the work inside the case causes him to step back slightly.

He swivels the chair toward him and sits, disappointed in himself.

He crosses one leg over the other, seeking resolve from somewhere within him.

He looks up, toward light, as though in prayer.

V/O: "—Ability to interview or examine witnesses.

—Ability to elicit useful evidence in a concise manner.

—Ability to act in an impartial manner."

His gaze turns toward the case, and his body follows, standing.

As he stands, he shifts the chair away from the desk.

He gently lifts the case, resting it slowly on its back, in ready position to be opened.

It's a daunting sight, and he backs away from the contents, landing at the mirror opposite the doorway.

He looks into the mirror and pulls on his face, trying to unearth how he got to this terrible place in life.

V/O: "—Knowledge of and sensitivity to Aboriginal culture and history.

—Knowledge of and sensitivity to sexual and physical abuse issues."

Reminded of his position and duties, he looks to the chair and resolves to conquer his fears.

He strides to the chair and jumps, landing standing on its seat.

He threatens the enemy in the briefcase with his own height, in battle position over the briefcase—one hand in a fist, one splayed at the ready

With no counter from the case, he stands up straight, newly bolstered.

He removes his tie, dropping it onto the floor like gloves before a duel.

Holding the chair back with one hand, he steps down onto the floor as into cold water, focus ever on the briefcase.

Bending closer, his hands reach low and around to seize the chair.

His arms swivel the chair so that it arrives at his legs, seating him firmly at the desk

The hands will not release from the chair to unlatch the case. He pulls. Pulls. Until his hands slam down onto the case—along with his head, which narrowly escapes hitting its sharp metal edge.

His hands flutter to the latches like frightened birds.

The latches open percussively, punching him in the face.

Slowly, shakily, he opens the case fully.

His hands become fists and his arms slump to the side of the case, then weighing further, down to his feet.

This pushes him back from the desk, head dropping low until he is bent over fully, head, fists, and feet all in a protective cluster, exoskeletal.

He removes the confining, hard shoes while crouched.

He slides them back behind him, through his chair legs.

Feet freed, he feels the suffocation of his suit jacket.

He struggles to stand and churns out of his jacket, coming to a kneeling, repentant position on the chair seat, arms hung over the chair back like a pew.

Slipping out of the arms of the jacket, he lets it fall behind his chair.

A moment of breath.

He grounds himself, sock feet on the floor.

Still crouching, he moves to face the contents of the case.

As he turns, his head touches the desk lamp and it lights.

The lamp becomes his companion, lighting the darkness for him. They look into the case together.

He takes plastic-sleeve-protected papers from the case.

He lays out the four touchstone papers on the ground beside the desk.

Light cuts through the papers, all in a line.

He brings out five grey, legal-sized folders and holds them close to his body as he latches the case.

He sets the briefcase on the floor beside the desk, opposite the papers. It, too, is cut by light.

Gently, almost apologetically, he lays out the folders on the desk, with each label showing. His hands tent over them, as he says:

HE: Children.

From the floor, the Compensation Rules beckon.

He picks them up and we hear him read as he walks:

V/O: "SECTION TWO: COMPENSATION RULES

Category SL5—Repeated, persistent incidents of anal or vaginal intercourse.

Repeated, persistent incidents of anal or vaginal penetration with an object."

He rounds the desk counter clockwise.

When he arrives at the lamp, he drags it along the desk to the downstage edge.

He crouches low to the floor, reading.

He reads in stillness.

V/O: "Category SL4—One or more incidents of anal or vaginal intercourse.

Repeated, persistent incidents of oral intercourse.

One or more incidents of anal/vaginal penetration with an object.

Category SL3—One or more incidents of oral intercourse.

One or more incidents of digital anal or vaginal penetration.

One or more incidents of attempted anal or vaginal penetration

Category SL2—One or more incidents of simulated intercourse.

Repeated, persistent fondling under clothing.

Category SL1—One or more incidents of fondling or kissing.

Nude photographs taken of the Claimant."

He flips the paper over.

Quickly, he stands.

He steps back fast, setting the lamp back on the edge of the desk.

He clicks the lamp off.

Backing away from the paper, he picks up his jacket and shoes.

He walks to the doorway as if to go.

He gets one foot partway into a shoe, and one arm into a jacket sleeve.

V/O: "CRITERIA FOR THE SELECTION OF ADJUDICATORS

—Law degree from a recognized university.

—Knowledge of and sensitivity to Aboriginal culture and history.

—Knowledge of and sensitivity to sexual and physical abuse issues."

He freezes.

He doesn't move. He looks rather like a broken umbrella, his jacket draping. He can't leave this important work.

He removes his jacket and drops it to the floor as he, himself, lands on his posterior on the floor.

He removes his socks and drops them onto the shoes.

He crawls to his tie on the floor and picks it up.

He moves to the lamp and turns it to face his face.

He clicks the lamp back on—spot-blinded, spine straightened.

He puts the tie on lamp, face to face. Colleagues!

Together with the lamp, he reaches for paper he had flipped upside down.

He picks up the Compensation Rules, carefully keeping it face down. He sets it on the desk.

Keeping a tight hold on the lamp, he walks around the desk to stand on the chair side.

Turning the Compensation Rules right side up, he holds the paper in the centre of the lamp light.

V/O: "Category SL1—Nude photographs taken of the Claimant."

He holds the paper down.

HE: Children.

He looks at paper again. He reads further.

V/O: "Nude photographs taken of the Claimant: 5 to 10 compensation points."

This has him recalling what the points translate to.

He sets the Rules paper down and reaches for the Application of Compensation Rules.

V/O: "Application of Compensation Rules.

1 to 10 Compensation points: 5 to 10 thousand Canadian dollars."

As he considers the text, he moves to crouch on the chair seat, folding up in horror.

V/O: "Category SL5—Repeated, persistent incidents of anal or vaginal intercourse.

Repeated, persistent incidents of anal or vaginal penetration with an object.

Compensation Points 45 to 60."

V/O: "41 to 60 Compensation points—51 to 85 thousand Canadian dollars."

V/O: "Repeated, persistent incidents of anal or vaginal penetration with an object: 51 to 85 thousand dollars." *(He repeats this, until he cracks.)*

Unable to rid the words from his head, he lifts the two pages, crumples them and moves them, with case, away from the desk and into a corner.

He stuffs the two pages into the case in the corner and latches it tight.

He sits on the case.

Gently, he looks toward the folders, checking in on them.

Quickly, he moves the glare of the lamp away from them.

He gathers the folders up and holds them close, shielding them.

He walks around the desk, away from the case, looking back at the case's contents as he says...

HE: Children. They were children!

He sets the folders on the chair seat.

Hugging the chair and folders, he pivots the chair so that the back of the chair blocks the folders from view of the case.

As he looks over the chair back to ensure the case is out of view, he spies the other two plastic-protected pages on the floor. Their contents come to mind and we hear them.

V/O: "Aggravating Factors: Add 5-15% of points for Act and Harm combined"

He moves toward the two remaining pages on the ground.

He picks them up, then stands.

HE: Act and Harm

V/O: "Verbal abuse

Racist acts"

HE: "Racist acts"—Ha!

V/O: "Intimidation/inability to complain; oppression

Humiliation; degradation

Sexual abuse accompanied by violence."

HE: *(Laughs of incredulously.)* "Racist acts!"

V/O: "Age of the victim—or abuse of a particularly vulnerable child."

HE: Children. Children!

He crumples Aggravating Factors and pins it with a foot as Categories of Harm begins to encroach and overlap.

V/O: "CATEGORIES OF HARM

Level of Harm H5. Continued harm resulting in serious dysfunction. Evidenced by: psychotic disorganization, loss of ego boundaries, personality disorders, pregnancy resulting from a defined sexual assault or the forced termination of such pregnancy—"

(Sounds of text, repeated and distorted.)

V/O: "—pregnancy resulting from a defined sexual assault or the forced termination of such pregnancy or being required to place for adoption a child resulting therefrom, self-injury, suicidal tendencies, inability to form or maintain personal relationships, chronic post-traumatic state, sexual dysfunction, or eating disorders."

He beats the pages against his body.

He shreds the pages.

He reaches through/under the desk and grabs the case.

He opens the case and stuffs Categories of Harm and Aggravating Factors into the briefcase, shredded crumbled pieces.

He closes the case, latching it.

He sees the lamp and brings it back into the act.

He aims the lamp at the case and accuses it.

HE: They were CHILDREN!

He sets the lamp on the floor behind him.

He smashes the case on the floor.

He stomps it with a foot.

He heaves up the desk and slams it down onto the case.

The case contents, at last, are quieted.

He flips the desk off of the case.

He slides the case far away, towards the door.

He checks on the folders, lowering his body to the seat of the chair where they rest.

He pivots the chair so its back shields the folders from the dead case, staying low, hugging the folders.

He crouch-walks over to the fallen desk with the folders held close.

He sets the folders neatly in a row on the ground, saying for each one…

HE: Child. Child. Child. Child. Child.

He umbrellas his body over the folders, on guard.

The thought of the case contents reviving is troubling him, so he seizes the chair, and in a swift attack, smashes it down onto the case.

He plucks his jacket from the ground and rushes to set it across the folders.

He picks up the lamp and does a slow scan of the area, a full 360°. In this, the audience is illuminated.

Satisfied there are no immediate threats, he sets the lamp down, lighting himself.

He sets himself at the "gate" of the desk and folders, as a guardian. He will not move. He won't allow the children to be further hurt.

END SECTION

Transition

Lights crash to black.

When lights return, the actors from Section 1 & 2 are on stage, not in character.

They set up a small kitchen table, two kitchen chairs, an easy chair, a side table with a framed photo and a lamp on it. After both actors from Section 2 have acknowledged him, Section 1 actor leaves.

The Section 2 actors face one another and agree when to begin, with a nod.

Lights crash to black.

Glen Gould as Emmett and PJ Prudat as Shannon.

Section 2: Daughter

A nice, though compact, condo.

There is a stylish accent chair, a kitchen table, two kitchen chairs, two used wine glasses, two cloth serviettes and half a bottle of wine.

SHANNON is wearing only her bra and underwear beneath a robe. There is a skirt and two stockings on the floor.

She pours wine.

EMMETT has all his clothing on, but it's in disarray. His boots are at the door.

After he buckles his belt, he picks up one framed photo from the side table.

SHANNON holds out a glass of wine to him.

SHANNON: Here. You earned it.

EMMETT: My god. I should be handing you a vineyard.

He sets down the photo and takes the glass.

SHANNON: The neighbours should. Miracle I stayed quiet as a mouse.

EMMETT: Flimsy walls?

SHANNON: Designer flimsy walls.

EMMETT: Ah! Mais oui.

SHANNON: So. Truth. Did you know my lascivious plans when I invited you here?

EMMETT: (*Laughing gently.*) Well, I… I didn't want to assume.

SHANNON: Was that too much?

EMMETT: I'm fine with it. Great with it. But I hope you don't do this often.

Beat.

EMMETT: I mean—I'd worry about you if… if you were my friend and you were having some strange guy over at your house? Some guy you met online?

SHANNON: Well… my friends know I'm armed.

EMMETT: Right. But just for hunting season, right?

SHANNON: Yeah, I keep it real traditional.

EMMETT: Me, too. Only for use in High Park.

SHANNON: Yeah! I like those smiling foggy ones. They just sit there. They make it so easy.

EMMETT: You mean those pasty white ones with the wannabe dreadlocks?

SHANNON: Yes! Only good after a good soak to rid of the gamey patchouli overtones, of course.

They laugh.

EMMETT: Stay away from the ones with strollers, though. Their young end up in sanctuaries, which is so sad.

SHANNON: Unless you snare them, too.

EMMETT: Oh! Cruel!

SHANNON: Sick and wrong!

They laugh.

EMMETT: Wow, you are… quite something.

SHANNON: Funny. That's what my dad always used to say.

EMMETT makes a gross-out sound.

SHANNON laughs.

SHANNON: I'm not calling you old. Or saying you're anything like him. I'm just… it's nice.

EMMETT: I'll just… take your word on that.

EMMETT picks up SHANNON's skirt and a stocking.

SHANNON: Oh, you don't have to do that.

EMMETT: It's only fair. You've been an exemplary host. The least I can do is clean up after myself.

SHANNON: So to speak.

He laughs uncomfortably. She smiles and throws her other stocking at him.

SHANNON : Well, if you're gonna pick up, you may as well darn this one while you're at it.

EMMETT: Happy to! Picked up some skills at school. I know how to make a meal with only a kettle, some powdered milk and the scowl of a nun.

SHANNON: You're like… the MacGyver of poverty.

EMMETT: Was. Hopefully those days are behind me.

SHANNON: Ya, tell me—Tell me about school.

A moment.

EMMETT: Okay.

She refills their glasses—only a glass or so remains in the bottle.

EMMETT: Are you plying me with wine?

SHANNON: I didn't need to.

EMMETT: Ha. Well—"In vino veritas."

SHANNON: Oh? What've you been lying about so far?

EMMETT: (*Laughing.*) You'll find I'm irritatingly honest. Job hazard.

SHANNON: A lawyer who can't lie. Wasn't there a Jim Carrey movie about that?

Through the walls we hear a crash of objects, perhaps in a closet.

SHANNON: Ah. Neighbour's home. (*Louder, directed at the neighbour.*) And pretending not to be eavesdropping.

EMMETT: They're gonna hear my big confession.

SHANNON: What's that?

EMMETT: Well, there is one thing I was… I am… surprised by… well, you're prettier in person than you are in your profile picture.

SHANNON: Huh. Not as pretty as you. Pretty little liar.

Emmett reacts.

SHANNON: You look younger than fifty-five. Way younger.

EMMETT: Well, I'm fifty-four until June.

SHANNON smiles.

She sits in the accent chair, well across the room.

Beside it is the small side table with the photos on it.

SHANNON: This is him.

EMMETT: Convocation?

SHANNON: Graduation. High school.

She holds the photo out for him.

He crosses to her and takes it.

EMMETT: He looks pretty proud of his little girl.

SHANNON: Always.

EMMETT: Cute. Nice hair. Good… height.

SHANNON: '90s magic. Hairspray and a blowdryer.

EMMETT: Wasn't that the '80s?

SHANNON: Shut up! It's the Soo *(as in Sault St. Marie)*. We were a little behind.

EMMETT: I admit. I am guilty of having feathered—I shouldn't throw stones.

SHANNON: Oo! I had a poster of Scott Baio above my bed.

EMMETT: And I had one of Valerie Bertinelli.

They laugh.

SHANNON: Wait. They let you have posters at residential school?

EMMETT: That was in uni.

SHANNON laughs even harder.

EMMETT: Well, we barely had any contact with the girls in rez school. So by the time I left… Valerie was much easier to be around than the real thing.

SHANNON: How things have changed.

EMMETT: Hm.

Silence.

EMMETT: So.

SHANNON: So.

EMMETT: Um. Do you… wanna go to a movie or something? Or for pizza?

SHANNON holds her hand out for the photo. He hands it to her.

She replaces it carefully.

SHANNON: (*Laughing.*) Like, we do the whole date in reverse order? Sex, a movie, and dinner?

EMMETT: Ha. I guess.

SHANNON: No. To the movie. I'd have to shower and I don't want to.

He begins to feel awkward as she gazes at him.

He sits on a chair at the dinner table.

SHANNON: I'm safe. Just so you know. I haven't been with anyone since my marriage ended. And I have an IUD.

EMMETT: Oh! Ya! Ya, me too. I mean—I got tested a bit ago, and… well, the only reason it might have been a question was because my wife—ex-wife… had been busy.

SHANNON: When were you tested?

EMMETT: Um.

SHANNON: Come on. Mine was seven months ago.

EMMETT: Last week.

SHANNON: So you did assume.

EMMETT: I hoped.

SHANNON: Ha. Good.

Beat.

EMMETT: (*Plainly, without irony.*) This is really awkward.

SHANNON laughs.

EMMETT: Sorry. I don't mean to be a kid about it, but… I guess I usually expect this kind of conversation to happen… horizontally.

SHANNON: Well. Sorry if I let you down.

EMMETT: God, no! Not at all. You're a trip. In a good way.

SHANNON: You, too.

EMMETT: Yeah? You're not...? Disappointed? Surprised by anything?

SHANNON: Disappointed—not at all. I'm surprised by how, I guess, shy you are.

EMMETT: Oh, yeah?

She moves to sit with him at the table.

SHANNON: Well, just... you're always posting new stuff on the page and sending out messages to the group about really... challenging things. But in person, you don't say much. Or, I should say, you don't instigate as much as you do online.

EMMETT: Bit of a coward without my qwerty, I guess.

SHANNON: No, no. Just... you're gentle. I always imagine activists are these loud, soap-boxing—

EMMETT: Well, I wouldn't describe myself as an activist.

SHANNON: Exactly! But I think you are. You're doing a lot to give voice to the people who belong to that support group. And I know it's just Facebook, so whatever, but—it's been a really good thing for a lot of people. People who really went through it. Like you.

EMMETT: Well. It's been... quite the process.

SHANNON: No kidding. There's something inherently fucked up about trying to apply a borrowed model to such a specific... fuck-up.

EMMETT: Yeah.

SHANNON: You'd think we would have learned by now that we can't import systems and try to impose them on issues that affect us here!

EMMETT: Yep.

SHANNON: The Irish boarding schools have some commonalities with Residential Sch… but why…? Our world views are completely different. God!

EMMETT: Does that count as soap-boxing?

They laugh slightly.

SHANNON: Sorry.

EMMETT: It's okay. It's kinda hot.

SHANNON: Look who I'm preaching to. What a dummy. I didn't go. My mom did. You did. I did not.

EMMETT: Let's order pizza.

SHANNON: You don't wanna talk about it at all, hey?

Beat.

SHANNON: School.

EMMETT: No, it's okay.

SHANNON: I didn't ever tell you…

He waits.

She struggles. She drinks. She pulls a second bottle of wine from a rack in the table.

SHANNON: Did I tell you my parents met at residential school?

EMMETT: No.

SHANNON: Yeah, my dad was one of the non-clergy who taught there. In, like… the early seventies.

EMMETT: And your mom was a student then?

SHANNON: He came in to teach welding to the senior boys when she was about to graduate. She was seventeen. He was only twenty, but still… I know. It seems kind of…

EMMETT: Imbalanced.

SHANNON: Nice choice.

EMMETT: And they...?

SHANNON: Got married the year after she graduated.

EMMETT: Wow.

SHANNON: She says they didn't start anything up until she left school, but... I don't know. Why would they stay in touch? Though she is really Catholic, so they were probably married before they...

EMMETT: Started up their patterns of passive aggression?

They laugh.

EMMETT: I guess that kind of thing happened a fair bit.

SHANNON: I was born there.

EMMETT: Holy shit.

SHANNON: I know! You know this Chinese belief that the place you were conceived affects your whole life path?

EMMETT shakes his head—no.

SHANNON: Well. I choose not to believe that, anyway.

EMMETT: I was born on the farm, in the back of a truck.

SHANNON: Like, a honey wagon?

EMMETT: Ha! No!

They laugh.

SHANNON: Does that, um... is it weird for you that my dad was... he wasn't one of the staff who... he didn't...

EMMETT: I wouldn't... no. "Weird" for me? I don't know. No.

SHANNON: You're not worried about sleeping with the enemy?

EMMETT: Well, technically you're only half enemy.

SHANNON: When is your hearing scheduled?

EMMETT: Not long. Summer.

SHANNON: Just in time for your birthday! WOOOO!

They cheers and drink.

A moment.

SHANNON: My mom didn't even want the Common Experience Payment. And that... that paperwork was hard enough. I can't imagine having to go through every assault, incident by incident and—

EMMETT: It's all I can do. We can do. So it has to be done.

SHANNON: Of course. And if you went through the worst...

EMMETT: Lots of people are... really paying for it. People get through the initial stages, to see if they're deserving of a hearing, but then it kills them.

SHANNON: Who?

EMMETT: What?

SHANNON: Sorry—

EMMETT: The survivors. Who start the Truth and Reconciliation process. What?

SHANNON: Mm, I read that there've been, just in B.C., there've been like, twenty-four deaths related to the Common Experience Payments? But, I mean, how can you calculate—

EMMETT: Always using numbers, aren't they?

Beat.

EMMETT: "Twenty-four." There's no way you can count that. Some people, it was enough just to have the forms to fill out. This one Elder back home, they made her fill her forms out four times. Same forms. Four times. Why?

She's got cataracts and English isn't her first language. By the time her money was supposed to come through, she was gone. I mean, the stress of it. It's delayed post-traumatic stress disorder. And there has been no move to account for that.

SHANNON: Mhm. And that's only on the one side.

EMMETT: What?

SHANNON: Well, your guy kicked the bucket. Right? You accused him, and blech! Gone. Before you even brought him to justice. Not that it's the same, but it's still part of the death toll.

EMMETT: The whole system, from day one, was set up to favour the oppressors. And too little too goddamn late, just like the whole fucking racket.

SHANNON only looks down.

EMMETT looks away.

Some time in silence.

EMMETT: I guess I do get "soap-boxy." Sorry.

SHANNON: It's okay. It was a way to try to get rid of us. We should be mad.

More silence. And drinking.

SHANNON: I'm not…for one second…implying that we should feel sorry for the staff who perpetrated such… fucking awful…

EMMETT: No, I know. I can imagine it's different for you. (*Beat.*) Maybe… if I ever meet your parents, we'll keep this on the list of things not to bring up at dinner, huh?

SHANNON: Huh…

He softens and checks in on her. He waits.

A moment.

SHANNON: Um. We lost my dad at Christmas, so it's fine, actually. But my mom may have issues with your smoking habit.

EMMETT: Oh. Shannon, I'm sorry.

A moment.

EMMETT: Are you okay?

She nods.

SHANNON: It's funny, after all these years, my mom moved back to the rez.

EMMETT: Yeah?

SHANNON: Yeah. I kinda couldn't believe it.

He smiles and waits.

SHANNON: She went through… she was one of those kids who actually found more calm at residential school than at home. Her home life was a fucking nightmare.

EMMETT: Shannon…

SHANNON: It's complicated, right? I mean… it's easy enough to draw a line down the middle and say that these people are to blame for what happened to these people, but… what about…? Who do we blame for what we do to ourselves? How far back do we go?

EMMETT: Go easy on yourself, Shannon.

SHANNON: My mom is… a real survivor, you know? Smart. So strong. But then her brother, who went through the same fucking childhood, is a… he's a…

EMMETT waits.

SHANNON: I mean, who do you blame for someone like him? If my mom managed to come out of it so good… who do you blame for a man who can do such things? To children.

Silence.

SHANNON drinks more wine.

EMMETT: Can I get you some water?

SHANNON: No.

She blows her nose on a napkin.

SHANNON: Thanks.

Beat.

SHANNON: "Truth and reconciliation." Jesus! Sometimes I wonder if it's worse now.

EMMETT: The truth always comes out eventually. It's just it's been pushed down so long that it's coming out all… backwards and sideways. It's—

SHANNON: Fucked up. And we're dealing with memories of stuff that happened, like, thirty years ago, right? At the earliest!

EMMETT: Yeah. Most of the people who were involved are dead already.

SHANNON: Yeah, and we're taking the word of people who are really really… damaged. You know? And the memory of a child is—

EMMETT: You don't forget something like that.

SHANNON: No, but you can scramble the details in your head. You can.

EMMETT: Shannon. I think maybe we should call it a night. I don't think we're talking about the same thing any more.

SHANNON: I can… We can talk about something else. Do something else.

He stands and retrieves his boots from the doorway.

EMMETT: Let's go see that documentary on Saturday, okay? I'll pick you up. We can go for Thai and then—

SHANNON: Stay, Emmett. Please? I haven't even put my clothes back on.

It's awkward and kind of awful.

He sits back down at the table.

They are silent for a time.

SHANNON: My dad was accused.

EMMETT is quiet. He doesn't look at her.

SHANNON: I know he didn't do it. I know.

She cries.

SHANNON: I grew up with him protecting me. He was somewhere safe, you know? Kind. Proud. That someone could accuse…

She cries.

SHANNON: I'm sorry. I'm so sorry. This is not a good first date. Snot is not sexy. (*She laughs.*) Ugh, I think I need to go to some kind of grief counseling or some shit. I'm sorry.

EMMETT: Yeah, maybe. If you feel ready. That's a big loss. Your dad.

SHANNON: Yeah. Can you…? Is it okay if I…?

She moves to his lap and wraps herself around him, crying.

EMMETT is uncomfortable, but he is too kind to resist. He comforts her…

She calms a little and then moves to straddle him—she removes his belt.

EMMETT: Shannon... Shannon. I don't want to... you're very.... I don't want you to do anything you'll regret.

SHANNON: How can I regret it? We already did it.

EMMETT: Shannon. You have tears in your mouth. It's too sad. You're very...

She gets off of him, holding his belt.

SHANNON: Sorry.

EMMETT: No, I. Shannon...

She drops the belt on the floor and picks up the remaining wine in the bottle.

SHANNON: You can go. It's okay if you just go. I'll see you online.

EMMETT: Shannon.

She looks at him.

He looks back.

Some time.

She sits back down in the accent chair, across the room. She gulps wine.

SHANNON: I'm sorry about what happened to you.

EMMETT doesn't say anything.

SHANNON: I'm sorry I mauled you. Nobody wants a crying girl in his face like that. Sorry.

EMMETT: It's okay.

Awkward silence.

EMMETT: I'm kind of outta practice, to be honest.

Shannon looks at him.

EMMETT: I haven't really been dating much. At all. For a while.

SHANNON: Too bad. So many women missing out.

He laughs shyly.

SHANNON: The walls here are actually surprisingly thin. For a concrete box. The floors are solid, but the walls are like paper plates. And the neighbour to the south is a nosey motherfucker.

She fashions a loop out of the belt and fastens it to the table then picks her skirt up off the floor.

EMMETT: What…? Are you doing?

She picks up her skirt and tears it. She throws it and her stockings to the floor.

SHANNON: I know who you are. Well. Your name. I've read your name. And I wanted to know who you were.

EMMETT: What?

SHANNON: My father died because you accused him of something he didn't do. His heart stopped. Because you broke it.

Beat.

SHANNON: "You don't forget something like that." It's true, but sometimes we get the details wrong, don't we? Don't we?

EMMETT: Shannon.

SHANNON: You saw his picture. You looked right at it. Held it in your hands. And, what? You didn't recognize him?

She pushes his face towards the photo. EMMETT is silent. Reduced to a young boy, abused at school. She releases him.

SHANNON: He died so hurt.

She chokes herself.

EMMETT: Shannon, what are you doing?

SHANNON: So fucking ruined by what you said about him.

EMMETT: Shannon! Stop this.

He pulls her choking hands from her throat. She moves away from him.

SHANNON: You have to take that back.

She tosses a chair over.

SHANNON: You have to retract your… your testimony about him. It's not true.

EMMETT: Shannon. Listen to me.

SHANNON: They weren't even gonna let him meet you. They make sure you don't have to see him. And it's so awful because if you had been made to look him in the eye, you would've realized you got the wrong guy. There's no reconciliation—only blame blame blame. And that. THAT is "imbalanced."

She takes his hand and punches herself with it. Hard.

EMMETT: Shannon!

SHANNON: NO! Rape is a stain. (*She spits blood at him.*) You never don't have it once it's been put on you. Whether someone lied about you having done it, or it happened to you, it's—But you know that, don't you? If it's true that someone raped you. DON'T YOU?

EMMETT: SHANNON!

She ties her leg to the table with a stocking.

SHANNON: NO! You listen to me. You didn't have to hear him, but you WILL HEAR ME. You don't fuck around with rape.

She swipes the wine glasses from the table, deep red splashing all over the floor.

SHANNON: Even that word. It's only whispered, it's so unspeakable. There's nothing that you can do to take that off of my dad now. My dad! Because of you. No.

She stretches her body across the table to secure a wrist to the table with the belt.

EMMETT: What are you DOING, SHANNON!?!?

SHANNON: HELP MEEEE!!!! HEEEELP ME!

PLEASE! PLEASE STOP! GET OFF ME!

She kicks and writhes and shouts.

EMMETT tries to stop her, physically.

He is trying to stop her arms and legs from flailing, being struck as he does.

A neighbor bangs at the door.

NEIGHBOUR: Shannon? Shannon are you okay in there? Shannon!

SHANNON screams and fights EMMETT until the apartment door is flung open by the NEIGHBOUR.

Blackout.

END SECTION

Transition

When lights come up, actor "Emmett" has helped "Shannon" from her bindings.

Actor from Section 3 mops up the red wine.

Actors from Section 2 clear furniture together. This is all friendly and warm.

Actors from Section 2 set up a single chair and a laptop and then leave.

Actor from Section 3 sets up a camera on tripod. A lamp is clamped to it.

When actor from Section 3 stands ready and still, the lights crash to black.

Jonathan Fisher in *Survivor*.

Section 3: Survivor

A sparse room, 2015.

A single gooseneck lamp clicks on, lighting the MAN.

There is a simple folding chair and a black plastic folio.

He is dressed neatly, shirt and trousers pressed.

He presses "record" on the camera.

Test. Test. Sssssss. Ess. Ess-words. Sssstephen Harper. Syphillis.

Puh. Puh. Parliament. Popo. Playback.

He watches the playback on the LED screen, listening through camera.

He adjusts his hair and tidies up a nostril.

He is ready to record.

PROJECTED: Behind him, we see what the camera sees, large.

He seats himself in the chair and tries to begin.

It's… I feel good, actually. Probably from deciding for sure. Always had hard times deciding things, then when I finally did, I felt better. So. I guess I feel good knowing. Was taught I didn't know anything. Couldn't know. Only memorize and repeat. "Our father who aren't in heaven…" "Yes, father. Thank you father."

I come outta the Pen and I knew. Knew what I wanted to do for work. Learned a bunch of IT stuff, then HTML from there, and now this. Feels good to know we have the best website of probably any band. Proud of the youth forum on here, too. That's my nephew who does the online ambassador stuff, you know. Charlie? You all know, but I mean... everyone else.

Got sober, too. But youse know that, too. Sick of hearing it. Doesn't take much to get on peoples' nerves at a party. All you gotta do is NOT have a beer and POOF! you're an asshole. Sorry, Mom. If you see this. Probably won't want to. All I can say about that is that it got me back to the start. Before any of the stealing happened. Little little kid and I knew some things. Knew when the creek would run and when it would just be a soft silty trail. Knew who home was. Knew how to make my aunties laugh. Holy hell—knew I was funny!

Came outta school knowing only this—(*He shadows his eyes within his hands.*) like blinders. Couldn't hardly even see but nothing. Wanted basements. And back alleys. Dark. No sound. No breath. Just nothing. And I run after it. And I got it. Slammed down so much rye whiskey it didn't matter that I didn't know.

When prison finally stuck, that's when I started knowing again. Had to be sober. Had to wake up. Have light. See. Hear.

Beat.

Beat.

That wasn't part of it—remembering all the school stuff. Nobody wants to remember or say any of that.

You know the first thing they done when we got there was make sure we didn't talk. Not just not talk our home language, but not talk at all. To each other. To ourselves. Hardly talk at all except when they make us all say the same thing, all together in a room too big for anyone to hear. And that's how they steal voices. Because voices are…

All I remember about Dad was his voice and his flannel shirt, right here. (*Close against his cheek.*) Tobacco smell. Chair pulled up right by the stove. Me, small. Sitting there. Listening through his ribs.

Came back from that first year and he was gone. First time at the cemetery, and the wind tore through my coat. Screamed all around my head, trying real hard to whip up my hair. Short, though. Almost too short to get messy. Grannie give me his cup to bring out. Asked her why the wind was so mad. You said maybe we shouldn't be there. But really we thought probably God was mad at her, talking Indian even though we were talking to her in English. And then she said, in English, "That's our ancestors, asking to be heard." Then she said it again in Indian and that wind eased up and went soft. Smelled warm. 'Member? Wood smoke and tobacco. And for the first time since the first week in school, I heard Dad's voice in my head. Clear and low.

They get us to tell them all the things that happened there. They write it down. Type it. Record it. Ask more questions. Like being at the doctor, only more like the zoo. Guess that's why those bears look so miserable.

Took Charlie there when he was about seven. Eight? My nephew. You remember, Chuck? Piled in your mom's truck with all your stuffed animals. Wanted to find each one, in person, at the zoo. Damned if I didn't carry those things around all afternoon. And bought you three more once we was there. We found them, too. Most of them. No luck with the orange and blue zebra. But you were so excited, anyways. Then I went and lost your giraffe. Shoulda put them in a big bag, but you said they'd smother. Looked everywhere for that damn thing. Probably some other kid found it and didn't mind how sticky it was. You tried to stay cool, but you got so tired and you finally just cried and cried. Had to carry you and the rest of your zoo back to the truck. You zonked out before we even made it to the parking lot. So wrecked. Felt so bad.

I put your whole zoo on the boot mat—soft landing—and laid you down on top of them. Set my coat on you. Turned on the oldies and headed home.

Silence.

Went to the bar instead. "Just for one." Felt bad. 'Cause of a giraffe. Two, three hours later, some lady comes in with you, says she found you wandering in the parking lot. You looked so small. Scared. Took ten more years of doing dumb shit before I got clean. Sorry, Chuck. Such a sweet fuckin' kid. Even now. Young man, though. Of course. Sorry. Every time I looked at you I wished I had my own kids and so glad I didn't. Screw up. Everything. Almost. Tell your mom I'm sorry, too. I know she won't watch this.

Don't even like that expression, actually. "Clean." You have a drink, I don't care. You smoke a J, help yourself. Long as it's not around kids, you know? Don't make you dirty. Me, though… made me far. From myself. Sends me off somewheres, dunno where. Realized one day, what if I don't come back? Rez school, hospital, prison… been lots of shitty places, and I always made it back. 'Cause I could see where I was and where was home. But drunk? No idea. What I like to say, actually, is I'm clear now. But people don't get that. It's not a catchphrase. Or if it is, it ain't so catchy.

Anyways… I know you guys don't like that talk.

You got all the passwords, Charlie. For the site updates and that. Email. You got all the skills, you can do my job, easy. If you want it. I know you're a talker, though, so you might want something a bit more social and that. Anyway… You just do whatever you want. I opened an account for you at the Credit Union. For school. I know your mom started one for you, but I don't know where. So, I'll send you that info, too. Sorry it's not more.

Most of the payout money I've used for funeral stuff and that. Mine. Cremation—sorry, Mom. No big event or nothing. Just… and paid for Mom's arrangements, too, for when she goes. Though that might be in a hundred years, so stubborn. Won't be too fancy or nothing 'cause I had to pay for my flight to Ottawa, and then arrangements to send my body back here. Don't worry—there's a funeral home guy will pick me up at the airport, so… but I guess by the time you see this, you'll already know that.

He laughs a little.

Grim sense of humour, hey? Us? Guess we have to.

I remember you telling me about the sanatorium, Mom. Like you were so lucky.

Got out of school young because of TB, and you talked about it like taking the satellite jackpot. Then you got real quiet. Think you felt a bit guilty, eh?

I'm glad, though—that you didn't have to spend so much time there. You're a good mom. And that's why Trina's a good mom.

Anyways… before I finish this up, I want to do something I never done before. Always wanted to. Too shy. Hell, I never even talked this much, never mind sing. But I wanna lead you all—everyone watching—I want to lead you all in the national anthem. Okay?

So… stand up.

He stands and tilts the camera up.

Stand up with me, guys, come on. A dying guy's wish, okay? So, come on. (*Beat.*) Okay, I would never force anyone to do anything, but if you want to stand and sing, let's do this. For reals. Stand up with me.

You know what? When I was at that fucking school, some boys didn't even know the anthem yet, and know what? Because of that, all us junior boys had to kneel on our boney little knees OVERNIGHT. ON THE HARDWOOD FLOOR. Boys ten, nine, eight years old. *We* knew the damn song by then—already been there a few years, us. But those newest boys? Some only five years old? They didn't know what half those words meant yet, never mind how to say them. Sing them. And we all suffered for it, so you can stand up for two minutes while we sing the National Fucking Anthem. STAND UP!

Okay.

He breathes deeply, finding his strongest voice.

And if you're gonna do this with me, I don't want nobody just moving their mouth, pretending to sing or nothing. Don't matter if it makes you uncomfortable or something—you think we were comfortable, staying awake all night on our knees? Getting strapped if we fell over for a second? You sing loud. If you don't care about those boys, you sing loud for hockey or Rita McNeil or whatever you gotta do. (*Beat.*)

Okay.

(*Singing:*) *"O, Canada! Our home and native land"* Pfff!

Beat.

"*True patriot love—*" that's a funny one.

'Cause I know "patriot" has to do with being patriotic, but I never did understand what love has to do with that. Maybe 'cause I never really did understand what "Canada" is. Nobody ever asked me if I wanted to be a part of it, but that's the name we got, innit? "Canada's First Peoples." Pfff. "True Patriot Love." Love I know. I learned about love in school. Learned I loved my mom because my heart felt how far she was from me, even though I had no idea where I was. Learned I loved my dad when his own hurt stopped his life short. Learned I loved my big sister Trina when I could see her across the dining hall, and my legs wanted to run over to her for one little minute to hug her and feel her hands on my hair. Remember where I come from. Who I was. I learned about love through hurt. Through not having. So, if being patriotic has to do with not having, I find that confusing because as far as I can see, "Canada" just takes whatever it wants, including kids. Anyways…

"*True patriot love. In all thy sons command.*"—whup! sorry, ladies.

"*With glowing hearts, we see thee rise, our true north strong and free—*" see, 'cause I got friends who live up north, hey, and they're strong as heck, but that idea about "free" is a little funny. They got a curfew siren goes off every night around ten. Government says it's to keep them safe, but you can bet your boots their kid didn't feel too safe when he got hauled in to the cop shop for being out past ten. 'Specially since his parents weren't told where he was for four days. They didn't rough him up or nothin'. He slipped on the ice. Got that black eye falling on a fucking snowbank or some shit. And ribs heal on their own, thank god. Cuz there's no hospital up near there anyway. Sorry. Okay—"…

true north strong and free." I think I get this now. This is a comedy song.

"From far and wide, O Canada, we stand on guard for thee!"

"God keep our land."—'cause there's people who think people can own land. And those same people tell other people they can't own land, and that the queen is going to go ahead and own that land for them.

"Glorious and free!"—this is a good one!

"O, Canada, we stand on guard for thee..." and then the next line is just the same.

He's done.

He's quiet.

You can sit. I won't ask you to stand again. This ain't mass. Get comfy.

He retrieves some letters from his plastic folio.

Charlie. I'll miss you. I have this letter here for you. It explains why I done all this. The cops might want it, I guess, but there's another letter I'm sending you in the mail. That one's for you to keep. I'm doing this hoping you never will. Backward logic, I know. But the only Indians that seem to make the news are dead ones. Be pretty hard to ignore a dead Indian on the front step of your work, innit? 'Specially when you work on Parliament Hill. And I want to be heard. My whole life lived knowing my voice was taken. When I got that money I realized how to get it back. I been writing the government one letter every week since I had my hearing, telling them my plan. They know. Almost two years of letters. I sent them by paper and email, too, so it's all in my laptop. You keep that too, okay? And let the band know I want you to have my place. I'm gonna send them a letter, too, but... You never know who's gonna say what. Have a letter here for your grandma, too, because she doesn't like computers. Geez. This whole thing's been keeping Canada Post off the chopping block, innit?

Beat.

Then you would say "Old People Joke!" (*He laughs.*)

In the old way, it was a kid's uncle who was a dad to him. I hope I been that to you. Every happy thing in my life has been you, Charlie. All my goodness lives in you. It couldn't really make a go of it in here. Clear as I am, I know this to be true.

You live long and happy. But when those fuckers come after you, you come back at them strong. And don't swear. And quit smoking. It's real ugly on you anyways, you look like a moose trying to play a flute. And look after your mom. She always looked out for me. And tell her... what happened to me at school? Tell her...

He shuts off the camera and picks up his smartphone. He stares at his phone and then sets it back down.

He retrieves a letter from a folio.

So. Business.

Mkay.

He reads.

This video went live at twelve noon, June 21, 2015. At 11:30 a.m. today, on the steps of Parliament Hill, Algonquin Territory, I willfully consumed ten milligrams of fentanyl. The choice of this drug was deliberate.

I have committed this act of my own volition. All peoples mentioned in this video are oblivious to my plans, except for ruling entities who have been made aware and have never responded. This video is a statement about the lack of reconciliation I have felt during my experience of the Truth and Reconciliation Commission under Harper's Conservative government.

Beat.

I never voted for you.

Beat.

I give thanks to Murray Sinclair for leading, and to the Elders council of the TRC. You did your best, like so many others before you. We are where we are. Nothing we can do about that.

I timed this video to go live once I had died.—Have died. This site is hosted by a parent site I built. I deliberately disseminated this video to ensure erasure is extremely difficult. This won't be easy to disappear. And that's… that's the whole thing.

He turns the camera back off.

He sets up the video through his laptop, to post it online.

PROJECTION: A countdown. "This video goes live in 4h 59m 59s"

He picks his smartphone up again.

He calls up his sister's number.

CHUCK: Hello?

MAN: *(Surprised.)* Hey, Chuck. You're up early.

CHUCK: Yeh. Nobody else will take the early shift.

MAN: Oh! Good. Hey—can I talk to your mom? Don't tell her who's calling. No. Tell her… Tell her her little brother needs to talk to her. 'Kay?

CHUCK: Mkay. *(Further off.)* Hey, mom? Your little bro needs you, man. Phone!

Some moments pass.

TRINA: Hello?

MAN: Trina? It's your brother. (*Beat. She isn't speaking.*) I… Charlie sounds so grown up. (*Beat.)*

TRINA He is grown up.

MAN: Ya, I guess he is. (*Silence.*) Hey, listen. I wanted to… I wanted to let youse know I set a bit of money aside for him. For school. University or college or whatever he decides to do.

TRINA: Ya, he… we have an RESP. Credit Union.

MAN: Oh ya? Credit Union—ya, that's where I put this money. (*Beat.*) I can, uh… I can transfer it? Better, uh—interest and that, eh?

TRINA: Right. Yeah. Sure.

Beat.

MAN: Ya, I was thinking of when you applied for funding to get your apprenticeship.

TRINA: Ya. Don't want that to happen to my boy.

MAN: Ya, you never know what the peanut gallery is gonna decide.

Beat.

MAN: Think maybe they use that spinning basket thingy from the bingo hall.

They laugh.

TRINA: Nah, it's easy. You get funded if your last name's the same as the chief's.

They laugh.

MAN: Trina, I had to tell you something.

TRINA: Yeh?

MAN: What happened to me at school? It wasn't your fault. (*Silence.*) It wasn't your fault, Trina.

Clicking and shuffling, muffled sounds.

MAN: Trina? Trina.

A long moment of silence.

CHUCK: Uncle. Mom says come for pork chops.

MAN: Okay.

CHUCK: Are you coming to my grad? I get two freebies. Then I gotta sell some.

MAN: Ya.

CHUCK: You can have a freebie.

MAN: Cool.

CHUCK: Hey, Uncle.

MAN: Yeah?

CHUCK: Bring dessert.

MAN: 'Kay.

CHUCK: See yuh.

The click of a hang up.

The Man looks at his phone. Yes, he will see Chuck.

The man deletes the video.

Blackout.

Transition:

As the actor clears the stage, we are in darkness.

When the lights rise again, there is only one chair. An empty chair for all of the Residential School attendees who cannot be with us today.

END OF PLAY

A brief and incomplete bit of context on Indian Residential Schools

Indian Residential Schools (IRS)

The schools were created in 1879 to "kill the Indian in the child" due to the belief that Indigenous cultures, traditions and knowledge are inferior to Euro-centric ways. In 1884, attendance at schools was compulsory. Churches were given government funding per student as incentive to locate and kidnap children, and parents were threatened with imprisonment if they did not surrender their children.

Indian Residential Schools Settlement Agreement (IRSSA)

In 2003, in the face of many potential lawsuits, the Government of Canada launched a Dispute Resolution plan to compensate IRS survivors. Those amendments were considered extremely inadequate by Indigenous peoples. In response, the Assembly of First Nations launched a class action lawsuit in 2005 against the federal government. Rather than dealing with the hulking consequences of the largest civil suit against the government in the history of Canada, the feds signed the Indian Residential Schools Settlement Agreement (IRSSA) in 2006. Survivors were given the option to apply for the CEP, and IAP or opt out.

Common Experience Payment (CEP)

This was a pool of monies that could be applied for by survivors whose experience of IRS was not considered extraordinary. Any former student who was alive on May 30, 2005 could apply through official paperwork—no in-person aspect. Standard experience included kidnapping, unlawful confinement and corporal punishment that did not have permanent physical consequence as recognized by Euro-centric medicine. A survivor who participated agreed the perpetrating individuals would never face criminal charges filed by the claimant.

Independent Assessment Process (IAP)

This was for survivors who experienced sexual abuse or extraordinary physical abuse. As the official site http://www.iap-pei.ca notes, "It provides them with a way to settle their claim more quickly, out of court. The process is designed to be claimant-centred, but fair and neutral. It is an adjudication process. The Adjudicator resolves claims and awards compensation." The survivor had to testify to the abuse they suffered in detail, often for the first time. Again, a survivor who participated agreed the perpetrating individuals would never face criminal charges filed by the claimant.